G000122615

SPEECH ACTS AND PROSODIC MODELING IN SERVICE-ORIENTED DIALOG SYSTEMS

COMPUTER SCIENCE, TECHNOLOGY AND APPLICATIONS

Additional books in this series can be found on Nova's website
under the Series tab.

Additional E-books in this series can be found on Nova's website
under the E-book tab.

COMPUTER SCIENCE, TECHNOLOGY AND APPLICATIONS

SPEECH ACTS AND PROSODIC MODELING IN SERVICE-ORIENTED DIALOG SYSTEMS

CHRISTINA ALEXANDRIS

Nova Science Publishers, Inc.

New York

For permission to use material from this book please contact us:
Telephone 631-231-7269; Fax 631-231-8175
Web Site: http://www.novapublishers.com

NOTICE TO THE READER

The Publisher has taken reasonable care in the preparation of this book, but makes no expressed or implied warranty of any kind and assumes no responsibility for any errors or omissions. No liability is assumed for incidental or consequential damages in connection with or arising out of information contained in this book. The Publisher shall not be liable for any special, consequential, or exemplary damages resulting, in whole or in part, from the readers' use of, or reliance upon, this material.

Independent verification should be sought for any data, advice or recommendations contained in this book. In addition, no responsibility is assumed by the publisher for any injury and/or damage to persons or property arising from any methods, products, instructions, ideas or otherwise contained in this publication.

This publication is designed to provide accurate and authoritative information with regard to the subject matter covered herein. It is sold with the clear understanding that the Publisher is not engaged in rendering legal or any other professional services. If legal or any other expert assistance is required, the services of a competent person should be sought. FROM A DECLARATION OF PARTICIPANTS JOINTLY ADOPTED BY A COMMITTEE OF THE AMERICAN BAR ASSOCIATION AND A COMMITTEE OF PUBLISHERS.

LIBRARY OF CONGRESS CATALOGING-IN-PUBLICATION DATA

Alexandris, Christina.
 Speech acts and prosodic modeling in service-oriented dialog systems /
Christina Alexandris.
   p. cm.
 Includes index.
 ISBN 978-1-61728-972-9 (softcover)
 1. Human-computer interaction. 2. Natural language processing (Computer science) 3. Speech processing systems. 4. User interfaces (Computer systems) 5. Computer software--Human factors. I. Title.
 QA76.9.H85A535 2010
 005.4'37--dc22

Published by Nova Science Publishers, Inc. † New York

CONTENTS

PREFACE

Language-specific as well as culture-specific factors are observed to play a decisive role in User Specifications for spoken Human–Computer Interaction (HCI) Systems. This book determines and defines a finite set of re-usable, transferable and language independent specifications for prosodic modeling used as general parameters for the Speech Component in Human–Computer Interaction (HCI) Systems and, specifically, in Service-Oriented Dialog Systems, constituting an application field of HCI, usually directed to the General Public as a user group. Factors related to special applications such as emotion recognition, and/or special user groups, such as children or handicapped users, are not included in the present analysis.

Chapter 1

INTRODUCTION

1.1. SPECIFICATIONS FOR SERVICE ORIENTED DIALOG SYSTEMS

Language-specific as well as culture-specific factors are observed to play a decisive role in User Specifications for spoken Human – Computer Interaction (HCI) Systems.

The present approach targets to determine and to define a finite set of re-usable, transferable and language independent specifications for prosodic modeling used as general parameters for the Speech Component in Human – Computer Interaction (HCI) Systems and, specifically, in Service-Oriented Dialog Systems, constituting an application field of HCI, usually directed to the General Public as a user group. Factors related to special applications such as emotion recognition, and/or special user groups, such as children or handicapped users, are not included in the present analysis.

The present specifications aim to limit empirical prosodic modeling and to provide a general framework for facilitating both the construction and the evaluation processes of prosodic modeling, independently from sublanguage-specific parameters chosen for the System. The proposed specifications target to the features of Comprehensibility and User-friendliness in the spoken output produced by the System's Speech Component and to the overall efficiency and reliability of the System's performance.

The definition of language-independent and language-related specifications requires a framework defining the purpose and the intended user group of the HCI System. Systems intended for Experts are characterized by controlled input, while Systems with the General Public entail culture-specific factors and hence pose restrictions in regard to input. The intended user group determines the User-System Relationship, which is here defined as a basic parameter of an HCI System. In the present approach, the HCI System's purpose, intended user group and the User-System Relationship are related to the definition of the Speech Acts, the dialog structure and dialog content of the System. The dialog structure and dialog content are, in turn, related to the prosodic modeling of the System's spoken output. This set of relations is summarized in the following table (Table 1).

Table 1. Relation of User-group, the User-System Relationship, Speech Acts, Dialog Structure and Prosodic Modeling

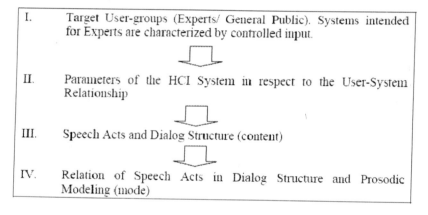

I.	Target User-groups (Experts/ General Public). Systems intended for Experts are characterized by controlled input.
II.	Parameters of the HCI System in respect to the User-System Relationship
III.	Speech Acts and Dialog Structure (content)
IV.	Relation of Speech Acts in Dialog Structure and Prosodic Modeling (mode)

From a psychological perspective, previous studies in Systems involving Human Computer Interaction (HCI), have demonstrated that the User is more likely to use the System and to oversee minor flaws if the System is user-friendly and if its spoken output is characterized by naturalness (Nottas et al, 2007). In this case, the User is also more likely to make the effort and gain the most benefit from the System's capabilities, disregarding the System's shortcomings.

1.2. THE USER-SYSTEM RELATIONSHIP AND RELATED PARAMETERS

The User-System Relationship is differentiated in respect to the physical form of the System (Base-Parameter 1). In particular, when the User communicates with a Robot, the User-System Relationship is different than the case in which the User communicates with a two-dimensional (2D) (or three dimensional -3D) Conversational Agent, appearing on a screen. In the latter case, applicable in the present approach, the Conversational Agent is virtual while in the first case, the System is real.

User-psychology may be considered an additional parameter determining the User-System Relationship. User-psychology (Base-Parameter 2) in respect to a System may be categorized in three basic types, excluding cases in which the User considers the System to be equal to a human, such as a friend or a relative. These three basic User-psychology types that may be identified are the following: (a) the System as an "Instrument" User-psychology, (b) the System as a "Servant" User-psychology and (c) the System as a "Pet" User-psychology. A User-psychology type, containing characteristics of the User-psychology types (a), (b) and (c) that may be additionally identified is the "Car Owner" User-psychology (d). The latter is more characteristic for "real" (tangible) HCI Systems like Robots.

The User-System Relationship is also effected by Task-type (Base-Parameter 3), depending on whether the System's function is (a) only the mechanical or program execution of task, (b) whether the tasks performed by the System are of the Service quality and (c) whether special tasks, such as entertainment and social company are assigned to the System.

Furthermore, the User-System Relationship is influenced by Language and Culture-specific parameters (Base-Parameter 4), namely on how familiar the Users are with the Systems and what type of language style and form of communication is expected to be used in the interaction.

An additional factor determining the User-System Relationship is the Initiative factor (Base-Parameter 5). In some Systems, tasks are initiated by the System and controlled by the User: the User's role is more that of responses, confirmations, approval and disapproval of the tasks executed by the System. In other cases, all tasks are initiated by the User and controlled by the System. In these cases, the System checks if the task is successfully performed and there are no errors.

1.3. BASE PARAMETERS OF PRESENT ANALYSIS

In the present approach, involving Service-Oriented dialog systems and interaction with a virtual speaker or Conversational Agent (Base-Parameter 1), we focus on experience gained from four European Union (EU) projects involving Speech Technology for social services and Human-Computer Interaction. Therefore, in the present approach, Language and Culture-specific parameters (Base-Parameter 4) are related to most European countries, including variations related to the Mediterranean. The EU Projects concerned include the SOPRANO Project (involving smart environments and services for the General Public, http://www.soprano-ip.org/), the HEARCOM Project (speech technology applications for Users with hearing problems, http://hearcom.eu/main.html), the ERMIS Project (emotionally sensitive HCI systems with Conversational Agents, http://www.image) and the AGENT-DYSL Project (involving speech technology applications and dyslexia, http://www.agent-dysl.eu/). Data is obtained from User Requirements Analysis in Work Packages, recorded data, questionnaires distributed to Users, dialog modeling corpora and studio recordings. We note that all the above-mentioned projects involve as a Project Partner the Institute for Language and Speech Processing (ILSP) -Athena Research and Innovation Center in Information, Communication and Knowledge Technologies, in Athens.

Table 2. Base Parameters of present approach

General Specifications: Base Parameters
(Base-Parameter 1) Physical Form of System: Virtual speaker/ Conversational Agent
Base-Parameter 4: Language and Culture-Specific factors: European (with variations)
(Base-Parameter 2) User-Psychology: (a) "System as an "Instrument" and (b) the System as a "Servant" User-psychology"
(Base-Parameter 3) Task-types: (a) mechanical or program task execution (b) service performance
(Base-Parameter 5) Initiative: "System-Initiative"

In relation to the above-presented Language and Culture-specific parameters (Base-Parameter 4), in the present approach, the following requirements are specified: a combination of (a) the System as an "Instrument" User-psychology and (b) the System as a "Servant" User-psychology (Base-Parameter 2) as well as the Task-types (Base-Parameter 3), specified as a combination of (a) mechanical or program task execution and (b) tasks of service performance quality. Following the typical strategy employed for achieving a maximum recognition rate in applications with highly varied user-input, as is the case of the General Public as a user group, the dialog is controlled by the System, therefore the Initiative factor (Base-Parameter 5) involved in the present framework is the "System Initiative" strategy.

The above-presented Base-Parameters (1-5) and respective features constitute the basic framework for the development and application of the proposed specifications for prosodic modeling. These Base-Parameters (1-5) are summarized in Table 2.

Chapter 2

SPEECH ACTS AND DIALOG STRUCTURE: THE SPEECH ACT-ORIENTED APPROACH IN DIALOG SYSTEMS

2.1. INTRODUCTION

In the present approach, prosodic modeling specifications are directly related to Speech Act type, determining the dialog structure and the dialog content of the HCI System. In respect to the framework of Service-Oriented dialog systems, Speech Acts are differentiated in (I) Task-related Speech Acts and in (II) Non-Task-related Speech Acts.

In Task-related Speech Acts, the content is usually standard and relatively language-independent. Furthermore, in Task-related Speech Acts, User expectations are predefined and also relatively language and culture independent. In Task-related Speech Acts a Controlled language-like approach can be applied to facilitate Speech Recognition and semantic processing and to standardize System input and output (Alexandris, 2009). Moreover, it has been observed that controlled language-like specifications originating from English (Smart, 2006, Wojcik and Holmback,1996) and German (Lehrndorfer, 1996) are mostly applicable in Greek (Alexandris, 2009).

In Non-Task-related Speech Acts, the content is often observed to be not standard, may be highly dependent on user-requirements and acceptable socio-cultural norms and is, therefore mostly language-dependent. Specifically, in the languages concerned, namely English, German and Greek, a balance between differences and similarities have been observed. In this case, a "lax" Controlled-language-like approach can be adopted.

Both the Controlled language-like approach for Task-related Speech Acts and the "lax" Controlled language-like approach for Non-Task-related Speech Acts presented here can be applied in Work packages for User Requirements and Dialog Modeling and may also provide a basis for prosodic modeling processes in other languages, apart from English, German and Greek.

2.2. RELATING SPEECH ACTS AND STEPS IN TASK-RELATED DIALOG STRUCTURE

Speech Acts for Task-related Dialogs (Heeman et al., 1998) can be related to utterances produced by a Conversational Agent in Dialog Systems. Specifically, in Task-related dialogs (for example, spoken technical texts), the content of the utterances produced by the Conversational Agent is related to the Speech Acts for Task-related Dialogs (Heeman et al., 1998) (Alexandris, 2009). The Speech Acts for Task-related Dialogs involve speech acts related to user-input recognition ("Acknowledge"), confirmation of user-input "Confirm", checking task completion/task success requested or activated by user ("Check"), providing user with necessary information or informing user about data requested by user, task success/failure or current status of process/system ("Inform") and handling of waiting time ("Filled Pause") (Heeman et al., 1998). The System may ask the user to provide specific input ("Request") and expect the user's response ("Respond") (Heeman et al., 1998). For reasons of efficiency, in many dialog systems, a considerable percentage of the questions asked by the System constitute "Yes/No Questions" ("Yes/No Question") requiring a "Yes" or a "No" as an answer from the user ("Yes/No Answer") (Heeman et al., 1998).

In dialog systems involving Task-related Dialogs, for example, spoken technical texts, steps in the dialog structure may be related to more than one Speech Act. Specifically, steps in the dialog structure involving the recognition of the user's answer and/or keyword recognition in user-input may be related to the "Acknowledge", "Request" or "Y/N Question" Speech Acts, as in the respective examples of utterances produced by the System (or System's Conversational Agent", namely "You have chosen the "Abort" option" ("Acknowledge"), "Please enter the requested date. Please press "1" ("Request") (Nottas et al., 2007) and "Do you wish to execute the program?" ("Y/N Question").

Problems in the processing of user-input and/or errors in the keyword recognition in user-input may be related to the both the Speech Acts "Check" and "Request", as in the example of the produced utterance "Input cannot be processed", "Your input cannot be processed. Please repeat" ("Check")/("Request").

Input provided by the user that does not constitute a "Yes/No Answer" or is not related to keyword recognition (Free input) can be followed by the Speech Acts "Check", "Inform" or "Request" as in the respective examples of utterances produced by the System "We assume that you have completed the process" ("Check") (Nottas et al., 2007), "You still have 30 seconds to file your complaint" ("Inform") and "Please add any further information you consider important" ("Request") (Nottas et al., 2007).

The Speech Acts "Confirm" and "Inform" may concern the closing of the dialog between System and User, as shown in the respective examples "Your entry has been successfully registered" ("Confirm") (Nottas et al., 2007) and "Your entry has been registered as No IE-6780923478" ("Inform"). Waiting time for the processing of user-input or for the completion of a process is handled by appropriate messages produced by the System such as "Please wait for two seconds" (Nottas et al., 2007), identified as a "Filled Pause" Speech Act.

Table 3. Relation of Step in Task-related Dialog Structure and Speech Act

Step in Dialog Structure	Speech Act
Answer / Keyword Recognition	Y/N Question
Problems or errors in Answer / Keyword Recognition Free Input Close Dialog	Inform
Answer / Keyword Recognition Problems or errors in Answer / Keyword Recognition Free Input	Request
Problems or errors in Answer / Keyword Recognition Free Input	Check
Close Dialog	Confirm
All steps in Dialog Structure	Filled Pause
Answer / Keyword Recognition	Acknowledge

Chapter 3

PROSODIC MODELLING AND SPEECH ACTS FOR TASK-RELATED DIALOG

3.1. PROSODIC EMPHASIS AND WORD CATEGORY

Prosodic modeling constitutes one of the typical strategies used in Dialog Systems (Kellner, 2004), contributing to the task efficiency and service efficiency of the system (Moeller, 2005). In task-related applications, for the General Public, prosodic modeling is observed to contribute both to the achievement of clarity, lack of ambiguity and user-friendly style (Alexandris, 2008), (Alexandris, 2007). For the requirements of the General Public as a User-Group, these targets are summarized as "Comprehensibility" and "User-Friendliness".

In the present approach, the above-presented Base-Parameters (1-5) and respective features constitute the basic framework for the development and application of the proposed prosodic modeling specifications, with data obtained from European Union Projects (English and German data) and National Projects (Greece).

In the proposed approach, prosodic modeling of all utterances related to the Speech Acts for Task-related Dialogs is based on the use of prosodic emphasis on the sublanguage-specific elements constituting the most important information in the sentence's semantic content, as well as sublanguage-independent elements such as negations and elements expressing time, space (movement), quality and quantity (Alexandris, 2009). Specifically, prosodic emphasis on the negations and elements expressing time, space (movement), quality and quantity is used for the achievement of Precision (Alexandris, 2008), while prosodic emphasis on sublanguage-specific expressions and terminology is used for the achievement of comprehensibility resulting to Directness (Alexandris, 2009).

In both Task-related and Non-Task-related Speech Acts, prosodic emphasis is used on the sublanguage-independent elements constituting negations and elements expressing time, space (movement), quality and quantity.

Sublanguage-specific elements receiving prosodic emphasis in monolingual and multilingual Task-related Speech Acts may constitute keywords grouped under ACTION-TYPE (Malagardi and Alexandris, 2009). These word groups involve expressions related to activities such as activating a program or controlling the environment such as checking if the power supply is turned off. Examples of keywords grouped under ACTION-TYPE are expressions contained within the Task-related Speech Acts and directly related to the execution of tasks such as such as "open"/ "close", "closed", "turn-on", "turned-on", "turn-off", "turned-off", "running", "start", "started", "stop", "stopped", "pause", "paused", "answer", "accept", "accepted", "reject", "rejected" and "lock" (data from the Speech Component of the SOPRANO Project, http://www.soprano-ip.org/). ACTION-TYPE expressions include keywords related to the Task-related Speech Acts but not directly related to the execution of tasks such as the expressions "understand" and "repeat". We note that expressions composed of more than one word that have to be processed by the system as a singular expression are presented with a dash "-" between the components.

In some applications involving multilingual Task-Related dialogs, prosodic emphasis may be used in sublanguage-specific elements that can be categorized as OBJECT-TYPE (Malagardi and Alexandris, 2009). Keywords grouped under OBJECT-TYPE comprise expressions related to objects involved in the activities concerned. Examples of such expressions are the words "door", "oven", "tap", "television", "lights", "air-conditioner", and, "thermostat". The keywords group OBJECT-TYPE also includes expressions signaling pre-defined small objects, such as "pill", or non-object-like entities such as "message", "dinner" and "phone-call".

Therefore, utterances in the System's Spoken Output constituting Task-related Speech Acts are characterised by prosodic emphasis given to at least two elements in the sentence, if it is considered that keywords constituting ACTION-TYPE are always related to keywords constituting OBJECT-TYPE (Malagardi and Alexandris, 2009), such as in the examples "The air-conditioner is turned on" ("Inform" Speech Act") and "Shall I vacuum the floor?" ("Yes/No Question").

Examples from recorded data from the Speech Component of the SOPRANO Project are presented in Example 1.

Example 1

Recorded data from the Speech Component of the SOPRANO Project. Short pauses are indicated as [Srt-P]

Speech Acts	
Example	Speech Act
"Do you wish to [Srt-P] **answer** [Srt-P] the **door**?" "Would you like to [Srt-P] **watch** [Srt-P] the **news**?" "Shall I [Srt-P] **turn** [Srt-P] **on** [Srt-P] the **dishwasher**?"	Y/N Question
"The [Srt-P] **air-conditioner** is **switched** [Srt-P] **on**." "The [Srt-P] **tap** is [Srt-P] **running**." "You have [Srt-P] **two** [Srt-P] **messages**"	Inform
"**Please** [Srt-P] **take** [Srt-P] your **pill**." "Would you like to [Srt-P] **watch** the [Srt-P] **news** or [Srt-P] the **sports section**?"	Request
I [Srt-P] **cannot** [Srt-P] **understand** you. **Please** [Srt-P] **repeat**."	Check

It may, therefore, be concluded that prosodic modeling of the utterances related to the Speech Acts for Task-related Dialogs is based on the use of prosodic emphasis on the sublanguage-specific elements constituting the most important information in the sentence's semantic content, as well as sublanguage-independent elements such as negations and elements expressing time, space (movement), quality and quantity (Alexandris, 2008).

Specifically, prosodic emphasis on the sublanguage-specific elements constituting negations and elements expressing time, space (movement), quality and quantity is used for the achievement of Precision (Alexandris, 2008), while prosodic emphasis on sublanguage-specific expressions and terminology is used for the achievement of Comprehensibility resulting to Directness (Table 4). These specifications may be incorporated in a general framework for controlling spoken output, similar to strategies employed in Controlled Languages (Alexandris, 2009).

For example, for the efficient handling of semantic content and/or for precision and directness in the interactions, the words "yes", "no", "packaging", "execute", "code", (sublanguage-specific expressions), "two minutes", "thirty seconds" (quantity - time), and "cannot" (negation) receive prosodic emphasis (in bold print) in the respective sentences from the CitizenShield dialog system for consumer complaints (Example 2): "SYSTEM: Please answer the following questions with a "**yes**" or a "**no**" Was there a problem with the **packaging**?", "SYSTEM: "Do you wish to **execute** the program?" (Speech Act: Yes/No Question), "SYSTEM: What is the **code** of the container?" (Speech Act: Request), "SYSTEM: Wait for **two minutes**" (Speech Act: Filled Pause), "SYSTEM: "You still have **30 seconds** to file your complaint" (Speech Act: Inform), "SYSTEM: Your input **cannot** be processed" (Speech Act: Inform/Check).

Examples from the Spoken Output Speech Component of the CitizenShield dialog system (National Project) are presented in Example 1. We note that all translations from Modern Greek are rendered with proximity to original syntactic structure.

Table 4. Relation of Prosodic Emphasis in Task-related Dialog Speech Acts and Purpose of Utterance

Parameter type	Elements receiving prosodic emphasis in Task-related Dialog Speech Acts	Purpose
Sublanguage -independent	spatial, temporal, quantitative expressions expressions related to manner and quality	Achievement of precision
Sublanguage -specific	Sublanguage-specific lexicon, expressions and terminology	Achievement of directness

Example 2

1. SYSTEM: Please answer the following questions with a "**yes**" or a "**no**". Was there a problem with the **packaging**?
    - (*Speech Act*: Yes/No Question)
2. SYSTEM: Do you wish to **execute** the program?
    - (*Speech Act*: Yes/No Question)
3. SYSTEM: What is the **code** of the container?"
    - (*Speech Act*: Request)
4. SYSTEM: Wait for **two minutes**"
    - (*Speech Act*: Filled Pause)
5. SYSTEM: You still have **30 seconds** to file your complaint
    - (*Speech Act*: Inform)
6. SYSTEM: Your input **cannot** be processed"
    - (*Speech Act*: Inform/Check)

In the languages concerned, prosodic emphasis is related to Comprehensibility and is observed to follow the same patterns in respect to word category that is emphasized. This may be related to the fact that in Task-related Speech Acts the content is fixed (standard) and therefore specifications tend to be more language-independent. This is confirmed by the present data from the above-presented European Union Projects. In this respect, the proposed prosodic modeling may act as a Controlled language-like approach applied to facilitate Speech Recognition and semantic processing and to standardize System input and output. Furthermore, it has been observed that Controlled language-like specifications regarding written and spoken technical texts (Task-Oriented Dialogs) originating from English and German have been observed to be generally applicable in Greek (Alexandris, 2009).

3.2. LANGUAGE-SPECIFIC PARAMETERS IN RESPECT TO PROSODIC EMPHASIS, WORD CATEGORY AND SEMANTIC CONTENT

3.2.1. Language-Specific Parameters in Greek

Previous studies have demonstrated a differentiation between specific word categories in which prosodic emphasis does not determine their semantic content (I) and word categories whose semantic content may be determined by prosodic emphasis (II) (Alexandris, 2008). In the first case, the semantic interpretation of the entire phrase or sentence may be determined by the type of element receiving prosodic emphasis, but the semantic content of the emphasized element itself is not effected.

The group of word categories whose semantic content may be determined by prosodic emphasis namely (1) spatial and temporal expressions, (2), a subgroup of quantifiers and numericals and (3) a sub-group of discourse particles identified as "politeness markers" (Alexandris and Fotinea, 2004) is classified as Category A or "Prosodically Determined" words (Table 5). For spatial and temporal expressions, and for the subgroup of quantifiers and numericals, the presence of prosodic emphasis signalizes an indexical interpretation ("exactly") as opposed to a vague (Schilder and Habel 2001), interpretation or a fixed expression (Alexandris, 2008), where in the latter cases, there is an absence of prosodic emphasis. For example, with prosodic emphasis there is an indexical interpretation of the spatial expression "'dipla" as "along" in the sentence "the crack was exactly along (parallel) to the band in the packaging" as opposed to its vague interpretation as "next-to" in the same sentence. The same is observed for the temporal expression "'oso" with its indexical interpretation as "for as long as" in the sentence "the array is created for as long as the loop is running" as opposed to its vague interpretation as "while" in the same sentence. Similarly, the numerical or quantificational expression "two" ("d'yo") is used in its indexical and literal meaning when it receives prosodic emphasis in the sentence "wait for two minutes", while, in the same sentence without prosodic emphasis, it is perceived as a fixed expression ("wait a moment").

For discourse particles identified as "politeness markers", the absence of prosodic emphasis signalizes them as politeness markers, while with the presence of prosodic emphasis they only have the property of discourse particles. Thus, absence of prosodic emphasis in the discourse particles "Tell me ('pite mou)" and "Mabey" ('mipos) signalizes positive politeness and friendliness towards the User in the following utterances produced by the Conversational Agents in Task-related Dialog Systems: Tell me ('pite mou), what is the product (Preferred utterance by Users), Mabey ('mipos) you want me to check the kitchen? (Alexandris, 2007, Alexandris, 2008).

**Table 5. Relation of Words of Category II to Prosodic Emphasis
(prosody and semantics of individual words)**

Spatial and Temporal Expressions:

o   Presence of Prosodic Emphasis = indexical interpretation
                                                        (= "exactly")
o   Absence of Prosodic Emphasis = vague interpretation

Quantifiers and numericals:

o   Presence of Prosodic Emphasis = indexical interpretation
                                                        (" ="exactly")
o   Absence of Prosodic Emphasis = fixed expression

Discourse Particles used as Politeness Markers:

o   Presence of Prosodic Emphasis = discourse particles, not associated with politeness
o   Absence of Prosodic Emphasis = discourse particles as politeness markers

The group of word categories where prosodic emphasis may emphasize or intensify, but may not determine the semantic content, is classified as Category B or "Prosodically Sensitive" words. This group involves (1) adjectives expressing quality and (2) adverbs expressing mode perceptible to the senses, used in a literal, non-metaphorical way. For example, prosodic emphasis on the adjective "round" ("strogi 'lo"), in the sentence "It was in a round box" signalizes the meaning "truly/par excellence round". Similarly, prosodic emphasis on the adverb "upside down" ("an'apoda"), for example, in the sentence "I turned it upside down" signalizes the meaning "completely upside down". Both Category A and Category B type prosodic emphasis may be used for the (a) correct interpretation of Speaker Input in the respective Automatic Speech Recognition (ASR) Modules and (b) for achieving user-friendliness in man-machine communication in the sense of "accuracy" and "directness" (Hausser, 2006) towards the user in the Conversational Agent's spoken output.

The rest of the word categories that are not effected by prosodic emphasis in respect to their semantic content are classified as Category C or "Prosodically Independent" words. The presence or absence of prosodic emphasis on words of Category C only effects the semantic interpretation of the entire phrase or sentence in which they belong. A significant percentage of these words are nouns or verbs and they may constitute sublanguage specific keywords. Prosodic emphasis on keywords focuses on the basic content of the utterance, for example, whether it is an action in question, in the case of a verb, or a specific object in question, in the case of a noun. Prosodic emphasis on the word elements of Category C, words is sentence dependent and highly sublanguage- and application-specific. Prosodic emphasis on elements of Category C is used both for (a) determining the basic content of the Speaker's input, (b) for directing the Speaker's input towards a keyword-specific answer, as well as (c) for achieving accuracy and directness in the Conversational Agent's output. For example, in the sentence "Please tell us any additional information you wish about the product or about your transaction" the keywords "additional", "product" and "transaction" receive prosodic emphasis for clarity towards the Users and simultaneously direct towards obtaining a respective keyword-specific answer, in this case "product-type" and "transaction-type". Similarly, a "Yes/No" Answer is requested with the use of prosodic emphasis either on "check" or on "thermostat" in the question "Shall I check the thermostat?"

In contrast to both A and B word categories, or "Prosodically Determined" and "Prosodically Sensitive" words, whose plus or minus ($\pm$) prosodic emphasis features can be systematically used in various Speech

Technology Applications, including Text-to-Speech (TTS) and Automatic Speech Recognition (ASR), the prosodic modelling of Category C or "Prosodically Independent" words is highly sublanguage-dependent and application-specific.

3.2.2. Prosodic Emphasis and Word Category in Other Languages: English and German

The above-described relationship between prosodic emphasis and semantic content of word and word category does not demonstrate a compatibility with English and German, at least in the dialogs in Service-Oriented HCI and in respect to the above-presented European Union projects. Language use (1) and differences in respect to morphosyntactical features (2) can account for a different relationship between prosodic emphasis and the above-presented word categories in English and German. In this case, prosodic emphasis does not influence the actual semantic content and, from an applicational aspect, may be classified as prosodic modelling of Category C for "Prosodically Independent" words.

Specifically, in regard to spatial and temporal expressions, quantifiers and numericals, in both English and German, prosodic modelling does not influence semantic content, in this case the indexical versus vague interpretation, and the indexical interpretation is achieved with the use of the respective adverbial modifiers. In particular, a wider use of indexical-type expressions is observed, either with the more extensive use of modifiers (adjectives or adverbs), for example "right above", or with the morphological structure and semantic content of the individual words themselves, for example "darüber" ("right above") in German.

Exceptions, however, do exist, in respect to the relationship between prosodic emphasis and semantic content of word and word category. For instance, some compatibility is observed mostly in American English in respect to the adjectives in Category B as "Prosodically Sensitive" words, for example the expression "big" (if receiving prosodic emphasis, may be equivalent to "really big"). It is also observed that, in a similar way to Greek, the presence of prosodic emphasis on English and German expressions partially equivalent to the Politeness Markers in Greek generates a rather unfriendly effect to spoken utterances produced by the System. For example, prosodic emphasis on the expressions "Tell me", "Please" or "Bitte" ("Please") in German, equivalent to the Politeness Markers in Greek, is observed to render them harsh and unfriendly, at least in regard to the above-mentioned data from the European Union projects Speech Technology for social services and Human-Computer Interaction.

It can, therefore, be noted, at least for the data concerned, that in English and German, in the above-presented word categories, prosodic emphasis is basically, used for emphasis but does not interfere with the actual semantic content of the expressions.

Chapter 4

PROSODIC MODELLING AND NON-TASK-RELATED SPEECH ACTS IN SERVICE-ORIENTED DIALOGS

4.1. INTRODUCTION

In Task-related Speech Acts, the Goal of the Human-Computer interaction is basically one, namely, the successful performance of the activated or requested task. In Non-Task-related Speech Acts, the Human-Computer interaction taking place is directed towards two Goals, namely (1) the successful performance of the activated or requested task and (2) User satisfaction and User-friendliness. The goal related to requirements on the Satisfaction Level in respect to a System's evaluation criteria, namely perceived task success, comparability of human partner and trustworthiness (Moeller, 2005) constitutes a basic issue in Non-Task-related Speech Acts.

It should be noted that the more Goals to be achieved, the more parameters in the System Design and System Requirements, and subsequently Dialog Design are to be considered (Wiegers, 2005). Prosodic modelling for the Non-Task-related Speech Acts may, therefore, be characterized as a complex task.

Table 6. Speech Acts and Goals in Service-Oriented Applications for the General Public

Task-related Speech Acts: Goal: (1) Perform Task successfully	Non-Task-related Speech Acts: Goal: (1) Perform Task successfully (2) User satisfaction / User-friendliness

4.2. DEFINING NON-TASK-RELATED SPEECH ACTS IN DIALOG STRUCTURE

Data from European Union projects in Speech Technology for social services and Human-Computer Interaction in English, German and Greek allows the formulation of a general categorization scheme of Non-Task-related Speech Acts. Specifically, Non-Task-related Speech Acts can be divided into three main categories: Speech Acts constituting an independent step in dialog structure (Category 1), Speech Acts attached to other Speech Acts constituting with them a singular step in dialog structure (Category 2) and Speech Acts constituting an optional step in dialog structure in Service-Oriented dialogs (Category 3). Speech Acts of Category 3 constitute a marginal category, between Non-Task-related Speech Acts and the strictly Task-related Speech Acts.

Non-Task-related Speech Acts of Category 1 involve the (1.1) "Open Dialog-Greeting" and (1.2) the "Close Dialog" Speech Acts. Examples of Non-Task-related Speech Acts of Category 1 are the utterances "Hello" ("Open Dialog-Greeting") and "Thank you for using the Quick-Serve Interface" ("Close Dialog").

Non-Task-related Speech Acts of Category 2 attached to other Speech Acts are the Speech Acts related to the "Error" concept (2.1), namely (a) "Apologize", and (b) "Justify", the Speech Act "Introduce-new-task" (2.2) and Speech Acts related to the "Delay" concept (2.3), namely (a) "Inform-delay" and (b) "Manage-waiting-time".

Examples of Speech Acts in Category 2.1 are utterance (a) "I am sorry" ("Apologize") following or preceeding the Task-Related Speech Act ("Inform"): "Your input cannot be processed", utterance (b) "I cannot understand your request" ("Justify") following or preceeding the Task-Related Speech Act ("Request"): "Please repeat". An example of the "Introduce-new-task" Speech Act (2.2.) is the utterance "To provide better services for you, I will ask you a few more questions." ("Introduce-new-task") following or preceeding the Task-Related Speech Act ("Y/N Question"): "Would you like to create a member's account?" Examples of Speech Acts in Category 2.3 are utterance (a) "This might take a few seconds" ("Inform-delay") following or preceeding the Task-Related Speech Act ("Filled pause"): "Please wait. Your input is being processed", and utterance (b) "Do you wish to proceed?" ("Manage-waiting-time") following or preceeding the Task-Related Speech Act ("Filled pause"): "If you have finished with your input, please press OK".

A Non-Task-related Speech Act of Category 2 that usually follows a Task-related Speech Act is the "Thank" Speech Act (2.4). Typical examples of the "Thank" Speech Act are the utterances "Thank you for your input" and "Thank you for using Quick-Serve". We note that the "Thank" Speech Act may in some cases be optional and that in other cases it may coincide with the "Close-Dialog" Speech Act (1.2). A Non-Task-related Speech Act of Category 2, that usually preceeds a Task-related Speech Act is the "Attention-alert" Speech Act (2.5), alerting the User on the content of the Task-related Speech Act that is going to follow. Similarly to the "Thank" Speech Act, the use of the "Attention-alert" Speech Act is optional and dependent on User Requirements (for example, Elderly Users, with hearing problems or/and a tendency to forgetfulness). The "Attention-alert" Speech Act may involve the calling of the User's name or the production of utterances requiring the User's attention such as "Attention" and "Mr. X, this is important".

Non-Task-related Speech Acts of Category 3, constituting optional step in dialog structure in Service-Oriented dialogs, involve the Speech Acts related to the "Optional-Information" concept (3.1), namely the (a) "Offer" and (b) the "Reminder" Speech Acts. An additional Speech Act type that may be classified under Category 3 is the "Initiate-Conversation" Speech Act (3.2). In the Non-Task-related Speech Acts of Category 3, the System may take its own initiative and "barge in" the standard dialog. Non-Task-related Speech Acts of Category 3 are optional steps in dialog structure and are directly dependent on User-Requirements.

Examples of Speech Acts in Category 3.1 are utterance (a) "Let me assist you with this process" ("Offer") and utterance (b) ("Reminder") "You still have two minutes to complete this transaction". The "Initiate-Conversation" Speech Act may ask the User if additional information is requested in topics such as the weather and news reports. Additionally, the "Initiate-Conversation" Speech Act may also be used as a form of managing waiting time by receiving free input by the User, which may be then filed in the System's database. For example, the System may ask "Please tell me what you believe must be done to improve our services?"

Finally, it should be noted that variations or more specialized subsets of the present Non-Task-related Speech Acts categorization may be identified, according to HCI System type and User Requirements. Furthermore, possible additional categories may be included.

All Non-Task-related Speech Acts are presented in Table 7.

Table 7. Non-Task-related Speech Acts

Category 1:
Speech Acts constituting independent step in dialog structure

(1.1) "Open Dialog-Greeting"
(1.2) "Close Dialog"

Category 2:
Speech Acts attached to other Speech Acts

(2.1) "Error"
    (a) "Apologize"
    (b) "Justify"

(2.2) "Introduce-new-task"

(2.3) "Delay"
    (a) "Inform-delay"
    (b) "Manage-waiting-time"

(2.4) "Thank"

(2.5) "Attention-alert"

4.3. PROSODIC MODELING AND NON-TASK-RELATED SPEECH ACTS IN SERVICE-ORIENTED APPLICATIONS

4.3.1. Introduction

Prosodic modeling for utterances produced by the Conversational Agent constituting Non-Task-related Speech Acts, namely Speech Acts that are not directly related to the Speech Acts for Task-related Dialogs, are observed not to be entirely empirical, although they are highly dependent on the style and type of Conversational Agents chosen for an HCI system. Specifically, it has been observed that some elements related to User-friendliness are not system-specific and can be transferred to other HCI applications involving Service-Oriented dialog systems.

4.3.2. Prosodic Modeling and the User-System Relationship In Greek

It has been observed that for languages like Greek, where friendliness is related to directness and spontaneity, constituting features of Positive Politeness (Sifianou, 2001), from a prosodic aspect, User-friendliness can be achieved with prosodic emphasis on expressions related to the User-System Relationship. These types of expressions can be subsumed under the general category of expressions involving the System's or User's positive intention or cooperation and may be related to respective Speech Acts.

Thus, the focus is given on the content of the Non-Task-related Speech Acts based on the User-System Relationship. This is unlike the standard content of Task-related Speech Acts, which, in contrast, focus on the actual task to be executed.

Specifically, in Greek Service-oriented HCI applications, prosodic emphasis is given on words signalizing the User-System Relationship ("Usr-Sys-Rel" words), namely verbs expressing the system's intention (action) to serve the user, expressions (usually verbs) indicating the system's apologies, failure or error in respect to a task executed to serve the user, verbs expressing the user's actions or intentions, nouns expressing a task related to the actual interaction involving good intentions ("cooperation") and nouns expressing a task related to the system's services. These word categories may be described as expressions related to the System's positive attitude toward the User.

In the following examples (Example 2 and Example 3) from the CitizenShield dialog system (Nottas el al, 2007), the above listed types of words signalizing the User-System Relationship receive prosodic emphasis ("Usr-Sys-Rel prosodic emphasis", indicated in bold print). These words are the expressions "sorry" (system-intention noun – in Greek), "ask" (Greek: "make"), (system-service verb), "thank" (system-intention verb) and "completed" (user-action verb). At this point, it is important to stress that not all Non-Task-related Speech Acts necessarily contain "Usr-Sys-Rel" expressions.

It should, additionally, be noted that expressions signalizing negations, temporal and spatial information, quantity and quality, as well as sublanguage-specific task-related expressions categorized under "ACTION-TYPE" and "OBJECT-TYPE" (as demonstrated in 3.1) receive prosodic emphasis by default ("default prosodic emphasis", indicated in italics). In Example 3, these are the expressions "not", "some", "correctly", "very much", "more" and "additional" (Alexandris, 2007).

Example 3

1. *Δεν* είμαι *σίγουρος* ότι κατάλαβα *σωστά* ("Justify")
2. *Συγγνώμη δεν* σας *άκουσα* ("Justify")
3. Θα σας **κάνω** *μερικές* ερωτήσεις *ακόμα* ("Introduce-new-task")
4. Σας **ευχαριστούμε** *πολύ* για την **συνεργασία** σας ("Thank")
5. Σας **ευχαριστώ** για τα *επιπλέον* στοιχεία ("Thank")
6. *Προφανώς* ολοκληρώσατε με τις *επιπλέον* πληροφορίες ("Reminder")

Translations close to the syntax of original spoken utterances

1. I am *not* **sure** that I understood *correctly* ("Justify")
2. I am **sorry**, I could *not hear* you. ("Justify")
3. I will (Greek: **make**) you *some more* questions ("Introduce-new-task")
4. We **thank you** *very much* for your **cooperation** ("Thank")
5. I **thank you** for the *additional* information ("Thank")
6. You have *obviously* **completed** providing the *additional* input ("Reminder")

Therefore, in contrast to Task-related Speech Acts where Prosodic Emphasis for Prosodic Modeling is given to keywords from the Sublanguage-specific lexicon, expressions and terminology, in Non-Task-related Speech Acts, Prosodic Emphasis for Prosodic Modeling is additionally given to specific Word-groups, signalizing the User-System Relationship namely (1) system-service verbs, (2) system-intention verbs, (3) system-service nouns, (4) system-intention nouns, (5) user-intention verbs and (5) user-action verbs. We note that, in accordance to the complex nature of the Goals that need to be reached in Non-Task-related Speech Acts, prosodic modeling specifications are equally complex.

- Relation of "Usr-Sys-Rel prosodic emphasis" and "default prosodic emphasis"

Additionally, it should be stressed that in Non-Task-related Speech Acts, "Usr-Sys-Rel prosodic emphasis" has a priority over "default prosodic emphasis" in respect to amplitude. Specifically, in Non-Task-related Speech Acts, the amplitude of the prosodic emphasis on Usr-Sys-Rel expressions is intended to be slightly higher than the amplitude of the prosodic emphasis on expressions receiving default prosodic emphasis. This specification is in accordance with the Goal of User Satisfaction and User-friendliness for Non-Task-related Speech Acts presented in Table 6. We also note that the above-described features constitute basic specifications and are subject to further "streamlining" when processed by prosodic modeling tools.

The sublanguage-specific User-System Relationship Word groups observed in Greek Service-oriented HCI applications are presented in Table 8.

Table 8. User-System Relationship Word Groups (Greek):

Verbs:
(1) verbs expressing the system's intention (action) to serve the user
(system-service verbs)

(2) verbs expressing the system's apologies, failure or error in respect to a task executed to serve the user   (system-intention verbs)

(3) verbs expressing the user's actions or intention
(user-action/intention verbs)

Nouns:
(4) nouns expressing a task related to the actual interaction involving good intentions (i.e. "cooperation")   (system-intention nouns)

(5) nouns expressing a task related to the related to the system's services
(system-service nouns)

Beyond the above-presented framework, it may be added that, in the Non-Task-related Speech Act "Attention-alert" (Category 2.5), prosodic emphasis is also given to a small group of directives such as "listen" and "take" and exclamations, including the calling of the User's name.

In respect to the Non-Task-related Speech Acts of Category 3, for the Non-Task-related Speech Act "Initiate-Conversation", in which the User is asked whether information on additional topics is requested, a strategy followed in Task-related Speech Acts is employed. Specifically, in this case, prosodic emphasis is also used on small group of keywords signalizing information type, for example, "weather-report", "news" and "newspaper". This small set of words may be labeled as the "INFORMATION-TYPE" word group.

For the Non-Task-related Speech Acts of Category 1, it should be noted that Speech Acts of Category 1, namely, the "Open-Dialog-Greeting" (1.1) and "Close-Dialog" (1.2) Speech Acts, are mostly fixed expressions such as "Hello" and 'Goodbye". This observation also applies to all three languages concerned, namely Greek, English and German.

4.3.3. Prosodic Modeling and the User-System Relationship in English and German

Despite the fact that English and German are not characterized by Positive Politeness, expressions signaling the User-System Relationship (Usr-Sys-Rel) are observed to play a significant role in Non-Task-related Speech Acts, even though the above-described relationship between prosodic emphasis and word category in Non-Task-related Speech Acts is partially applicable in English and German. Specifically, prosodic emphasis on "Usr-Sys-Rel" expressions is observed to contribute to the achievement of clarity and User-friendliness in English and German spoken utterances in Service-Oriented dialog systems, at least in respect to the present data acquired from European Union projects in Speech Technology for social services and Human-Computer Interaction.

Examples of respective expressions receiving prosodic emphasis in HCI applications in English and in German from data received from European Union Projects (i.e. the SOPRANO Project, , http://www.soprano-ip.org/) are the words: "sorry", "apologize", (German: "entschuldigen") and "help", "assist", (German: "helfen", "behilflich").

We also note that words receiving prosodic emphasis (signalized in bold writing) by default, namely negation, spatial, temporal, quantitative expressions and expressions related to manner and quality as well as sublanguage-specific task-related expressions categorized under "ACTION-TYPE" and "OBJECT-TYPE" (as demonstrated in 3.1) receive prosodic emphasis by default ("default prosodic emphasis"). Default prosodic emphasis is henceforth indicated in italics.

Prosodic modeling in English and German may produce similar examples in the two languages, in case a translation similar to a word-to-word translation of the previous (Greek) examples is performed. Usr-Sys-Rel expressions in English and German may correspond to the same or to a different grammatical category in relation to Greek Usr-Sys-Rel expressions. For example, a Usr-Sys-Rel expression in Greek may constitute a system-service-verb, while in English or in German the equivalent expression may constitute a system-service-noun. We also note that, similarly to Greek, not all Non-Task-related Speech Acts necessarily contain Usr-Sys-Rel expressions.

The sublanguage-specific User-System Relationship Word groups observed in English and German Service-oriented HCI applications are presented in Table 9.

Table 9. Prosodic Emphasis in User-System Relationship Word groups (Usr-Sys-Rel) (German and English)

(1) expressions (nouns/verbs/adjectives) indicating the system's intention (action) to serve the user / a task related to the related to the system's services   (system-service expressions)
(2) expressions (nouns/verbs/adjectives) indicating the system's apologies, failure or error in respect to a task executed to serve the user / a task related to the actual interaction involving good intentions   (system-intention expressions)
(3) expressions (nouns/verbs/adjectives) indicating the user's actions or intentions   (user-action/intention expressions)

In the respective English and German examples that will be presented, all words related to the User-System Relationship (Usr-Sys-Rel) and therefore receive prosodic emphasis are signalized in bold writing, regardless of their grammatical category. Usr-Sys-Rel expressions in English and German compatible with the respective above-presented Greek utterances are illustrated by the following examples of Category 2 in English and German (Example 4 and Example 5).

We note that, similarly to Greek, in English and German Non-Task-related Speech Acts, the amplitude of the prosodic emphasis on Usr-Sys-Rel expressions is intended to be slightly higher than the amplitude of the prosodic emphasis on expressions receiving default prosodic emphasis. Since the above-described features constitute basic specifications and are subject to further "streamlining" when processed by prosodic modeling tools, necessary adaptations are not symmetrical in the languages concerned and are also related to variations in syntax as well as in the vocabulary (lexicon) of the respective sublanguages.

Examples in English of Non-Task-related Speech Acts of Category 2.1 and 2.2 (Example 4) compatible with the above-presented Greek examples are utterance (a) "I am **sorry** (adjective)" ("Apologize"), utterance (b) "I **cannot understand** your **request** (noun)" ("Justify") and utterance (Category 2.2) "To provide **better services** (noun) for you, I will **ask** you a few more questions" ("Introduce-new-task") system-service noun, system-service verb.

Examples of Speech Acts in Category 2.3 (Example 4) are utterance (a) "This might take a *few seconds*" ("Inform-delay") and utterance (b) "Do you **wish** to *proceed*?" We note here that the Non-Task-related "Inform-delay" Speech Act presented here does not contain Usr-Sys-Rel expressions. Compatibility regarding prosodic emphasis and the User-System Relationship between Greek and English is also observed in respect to Speech Acts in Category 2.4 ("Thank") and Category 2.5 ("Attention-alert"), such as in the respective examples "**Thank you** for your **input**" (2.4) and "(Your) **Attention** (noun) please." We note that the expression "please" is related to pragmatic politeness and does not receive prosodic emphasis by default, as described in 3.2.2.

Example 4

(Usr-Sys-Rel prosodic emphasis (higher amplitude) indicated in bold, default emphasis (lower amplitude) indicated in italics)

Category 2.1
(a) "I am **sorry**" ("Apologize")
(b) "I *cannot understand* your **request**" ("Justify")

Category 2.2
"To provide **better services** for you, I will **ask** you a few more questions." ("Introduce-new-task")

Category 2.3
(a) "This might take a *few seconds*" ("Inform-delay")
(b) "Do you **wish** to *proceed*?" ("Manage-waiting-time")

Category 2.4 ("Thank")
"**Thank you** for your **input**"

Category 2.5 ("Attention-alert")
"(Your) **Attention** please"

Similar examples in German of Non-Task-related Speech Acts of Category 2.1 and 2.2 (Example 5) are utterance (a) "Ich bitte um **Entschuldigung** (noun)" or "Ich **möchte** mich **entschuldigen** (verb)"

("Apologize"), utterance (b) "Ich kann Ihre **Eingabe** (noun) *nicht verstehen* (verb)" or "Ihre **Eingabe** (noun) wurde *nicht richtig verstanden* (verb)" ("Justify") and utterance (Category 2.2) "Wir werden Ihnen *einige weitere* **Fragen stellen** (verb)" ("Introduce-new-task"). In the latter example, prosodic emphasis is given to the system-service noun and system-service verb "Fragen stellen". We note here that, depending on the specifications of the sublanguage concerned, the expression "Fragen stellen" may be either considered an Usr-Sys-Rel expression or an ACTION-TYPE expression receiving default prosodic emphasis.

Examples of Speech Acts in Category 2.3 are utterance (a) "Das kann *einige Minuten* dauern" ("Inform-delay") and utterance (b) "**Möchten** Sie *weitermachen* (verb)?" (user-intention verbs). Similarly as in English, compatibility with respective utterances in Greek is also observed in Speech Acts of Category 2.4 ("Thank") and Category 2.5 ("Attention-alert"), such as in the respective examples "**Danke** für Ihre **Eingabe** (noun)" (2.4) and "Ich bitte um Ihre **Aufmerksamkeit** (noun)" and "(Ihre) **Achtung** (noun)." Similarly to the respective example in English, we note that the expression "bitte" ("please") related to pragmatic politeness does not receive prosodic emphasis by default, as described in 3.2.2.

Example 5

(Usr-Sys-Rel prosodic emphasis (higher amplitude) indicated in bold, default emphasis (lower amplitude) indicated in italics)

Category 2.1
(a)
(i) "Ich bitte um **Entschuldigung**" ("Apologize"),
(ii) "Ich **möchte** mich **entschuldigen**" ("Apologize")

(b)
(i) "Ich kann Ihre **Eingabe** *nicht verstehen*" ("Justify")
(ii) "Ihre **Eingabe** wurde *nicht richtig verstanden*" ("Justify")

Category 2.2
" Wir werden Ihnen *einige weitere* **Fragen stellen**"
("Introduce-new-task")

Category 2.3
(a) "Das kann *einige Minuten* dauern" ("Inform-delay")
(b) "**Möchten** Sie *weitermachen*?" ("Manage-waiting-time")

Category 2.4 ("Thank")
"**Danke** für Ihre **Eingabe**"

Category 2.5 ("Attention-alert")
"Ich bitte um Ihre **Aufmerksamkeit**"
"(Ihre) **Achtung**""

4.4. LANGUAGE-SPECIFIC FEATURES IN PROSODIC MODELING AND NON-TASK-RELATED SPEECH ACTS

4.4.1. Introduction

As demonstrated from the above-presented examples, it may be observed that expressions signalizing the User-System Relationship play a significant role in Non-Task-related Speech Acts in English and German, as demonstrated from the above-presented examples. However, in the languages concerned, namely Greek, English and German, a partial compatibility is observed in respect to prosodic emphasis and expressions signalizing the User-System Relationship in Non-Task-related Speech Acts. Specifically, this partial compatibility in respect to "Usr-Sys-Rel" expressions is observed to be related to two basic factors, the Grammatical and Lexical Parameter and the Pragmatic and Sociolinguistic Parameter.

4.4.2. The Grammatical and Lexical Parameter

The Grammatical and Lexical Parameter may be described as differences in the morphological and the syntactic level and differences in respect to the semantic equivalence of expressions.

Differences in respect to the Morphosyntactic Level typically occur in verbs receiving prosodic emphasis and expressing the system's intention (action) to serve the user (system-service verbs), verbs expressing the system's apologies, failure or error in respect to a task executed to serve the user (system-intention verbs) and verbs expressing the user's actions or intentions (user-action/intention verbs).

In Greek, as a verb-framed and pro-drop language (like Spanish or Italian), the prosodic emphasis is directly matched to the finite verb, containing the features of the verb's subject - in this case the System or the User. This difference in respect to English and German may also influence the process of identifying Usr-Sys-Rel expressions.

For example, the Greek verb "'kano" ("I-do/make") in the context of "make questions" (in a literal transfer from Greek) (Example 6) is a primitive verb, containing the features of the verb's subject and does not have the task-specific semantics of the English equivalent verb "ask". Therefore, in the context of Service-oriented HCI applications, the Greek verb "'kano" may be identified as an Usr-Sys-Rel expression, in the sense that the System is "doing something" for the User, while the respective English equivalent verb "ask" is identified as an ACTION-TYPE expression. The German equivalent expression "Fragen stellen" ("pose/put questions"), the verb "stellen" contains more specific semantic features than the Greek verb "'kano" and less specific semantic features than the English verb "ask" and can be classified both as Usr-Sys-Rel expression or an ACTION-TYPE expression receiving default prosodic emphasis.

In another example, the Greek verb "olokli'rosate" ("completed") is equivalent to the verb "finished" in English, but with the adjective "fertig" (default-emphasis) in German (Example 6). We note that the semantics of the Greek verb "olokli'rosate" ("completed") allows it to be classified as a Usr-Sys-Rel expression, whereas the verb "finished" in English is classified as an ACTION-TYPE task-related expression receiving default emphasis.

In this respect, differences in the Morphosyntactic Level in the languages concerned may, in some cases, also be reflected in the semantic aspect.

According to the above-presented data, both in English and in German, the prosodic emphasis in Usr-Sys-Rel expressions and "default-emphasis" words (ACTION-TYPE) is observed to be directly matched to the finite verb, however, the subject is phonologically realized as a separate word. In this case, it may be concluded that the semantic feature of the subject is not included in the semantics of the emphasized Usr-Sys-Rel expression and that only the verb content-specific semantic features are actually emphasized. If prosodic emphasis given on the subject (pronoun, for instance "you" or "Sie" (German)), the result may have a harshly deictic effect.

The relation of the Morphosyntactic Level and the semantic and lexical aspect is also evident both in respect to the surface structure of the utterances and in expressions used. For example, in respect to the surface structure of the equivalent utterances, Greek verb "'kanete" ("do"), is equivalent to the finite verb "machen" ("do") in German, but with the verb "wish" in English. In a similar example, in the utterance "Please proceed", the Greek verb (Parakal´o –"please") "sine´xiste" ("proceed") is equivalent to the respective verb "proceed" in English, but with the adverb (Bitte machen/sprechen Sie) "weiter" (default-emphasis) in German. The relation of the Morphosyntactic Level and the Lexical aspect is also evident in respect to the expressions used, such as in the typically occurring examples of the "Apologize" and "Thank" Non-Task-related Speech Acts where the word category type of the Usr-Sys-Rel expressions is not always identical in the languages concerned. For example, apologies may be expressed with a noun in German and in Greek but with a verb or a fixed expression in English and the verb phrase "Thank you", a fixed expression in English corresponds to a verb-sentence in Greek.

Differences in respect to the Grammatical and Lexical Parameter concerning the languages Greek, English and German are presented in Example 6.

Example 6: Grammatical and Lexical Parameter

(Usr-Sys-Rel prosodic emphasis indicated in bold)
(1) Morphosyntactic Level:

i.   [.....] **ολοκληρώσατε** [.....] (verb = "[you] have-completed") – (olokli´rosate -"completed")
ii.   [.....] you have [.....] **finished**
iii.   [.....]Sie sind [.....] **fertig** (Adjective-default emphasis)

(2) Morphosyntactic Level :

i.   [.....] **κάνετε** [.....] (verb = "[you] do")- ('kanete" -"do")
ii.   [.....] you **wish** to **do**
iii.   [.....] **möchten** Sie [.....] **machen**

(3) Morphosyntactic Level:

i.   Παρακαλώ **συνεχίστε** (verb = "(you) proceed") - (parakal´o – "please") sine´xiste
ii.   Please **proceed**
iii.   Bitte machen (=do)/sprechen(=speak) Sie **weiter** (Adjective-default emphasis)

(4) Equivalence of expressions:
i.   Συγγνώμη (noun) (syg´nomi - apology)
ii.   I **apologize** (verb), I am **sorry** (adjective, with use of a fixed expression)
iii. **Entschuldigung** (noun)
        (5) Equivalence of expressions:
i.   Ευχαριστώ, Ευχαριστούμε (verb = "[I] thank", "[we] thank")) (efxari´sto, efxari´stume –"thank")
ii.   **Thank you** (fixed expression)
iii. **Danke** (fixed expression), **Vielen Dank** (fixed expression)
iv.   **möchten** uns **bedanken** (=wish we say-thanks)

4.4.3. The Pragmatic and Sociolinguistic Parameter

The Pragmatic and Sociolinguistic Parameter may indirectly influence prosodic emphasis in Non-Task-related Speech Acts. In particular, the Pragmatic and Sociolinguistic Parameter involves the differences between English, German and Greek observed in respect to the perception of the actual content of the utterances produced and differences in respect to the necessity or optionality of the actual speech acts.

In Example 7, the examples directly translated from Greek (the CitizenShield Project) "You have obviously finished with your additional input" and "I will ask you one more time" may seem too direct or even rude in English and in German. However, it is observed that, in Greek, the use of prosodic emphasis has a direct influence on the User-friendliness feature of a sentence. Specifically, in Example 7, the expression becomes polite if prosodic emphasis is given to the respective verbs "completed" (user-action verb) and the verb "ask" (system-service verb) along with the expressions receiving "default emphasis", namely, the numerical expression and the adverbs related to quantity "additional" and "one more". We note here that the effect will be harsher in the case in which only the "default emphasis" expressions "obviously" as an adverbial and "one" as a numerical expression is emphasized.

Example 7: Pragmatic and Sociolinguistic Parameter

(Usr-Sys-Rel prosodic emphasis indicated in bold, default emphasis indicated in italics)

Category 3.1 ("Optional Information": "Reminder")
i.   Προφανώς **ολοκληρώσατε** με τις **επιπλέον** πληροφορίες
ii.   Greek (in English): You have obviously **finished** (Greek: **completed**) with your **additional** input
iii. Greek (in German): Sie sind offensichtlich mit Ihrer **zusätzlichen Eingabe** *fertig* (Greek: **vervollständigt** – "completed")

Category 3.1 ("Optional Information": "Reminder")
i.   Θα σας **ρωτήσω ακόμη μια** φορά
ii.   Greek (in English): I will **ask** you *one more* time
iii. Greek (in German): Ich werde Ihnen *noch ein* Mal **fragen**

In Example 8, the System may in the case of Greek appear helpful to the User by introducing the new task, with the respective emphasis on Usr-Sys-Rel expressions. On the other hand, in English and in German, the System may seem too harsh and authoritative. We note that in English and in German, the addition of the adverbial "now" and "gleich" (German: "(right) now") seems to soften any harsh effect. In contrast, in the Greek example, friendliness does not appear to be effected by the presence or absence of the adverbial "now" ('tora).

Example 8: Pragmatic and Sociolinguistic Parameter

Category 2.3

("Introduce-new-task")

1. English:

- *I will ask you some more questions*
- *I will ask you some more questions now (Adverb)*
  2. German:
- *Ich werde Ihnen einige weitere Fragen stellen*
- *Ich werde Ihnen gleich (Adverb) einige weitere Fragen stellen*
  3. Greek:
- *Θα σας κάνω μερικές ερωτήσεις ακόμα – (Tha sas 'kano meri'kes ero'tisis a'koma)*
  o   *I will ask ("make") you some more questions*
- *Θα σας κάνω τώρα (adverb – "now") μερικές ερωτήσεις ακόμα – (Tha sas 'kano 'tora (=now) meri'kes ero'tisis a'koma)*

- *Τώρα (adverb) θα σας κάνω μερικές ερωτήσεις ακόμα ('Tora (=now)*
  tha sas 'kano 'tora meri'kes ero'tisis a'koma)
  - o *I will ask ("make") you some more questions now*

4.5. GENERAL OBSERVATIONS

As indicated in Section 3, in the present prosodic modeling framework, it is observed that in English, German and Greek, "default-emphasis" words, typical in Task-related Speech Acts, can be mapped to similar grammatical categories or word-categories. In contrast, expressions signalizing the User-System Relationship ("Usr-Sys-Rel" words) do not always demonstrate a full equivalence in the languages concerned.

Table 10. Relation of Speech Acts and Elements receiving Prosodic Emphasis for Prosodic Modelling in a Service-oriented Dialog System

Languages: English, German, Greek	
1. Task-related Speech Acts *Goal*: Precision, Directness	2. Non-Task-related Speech Acts *Goal*: Directness, User-friendliness
Sublanguage-specific *(task-related) expressions:* *Emphasis:* Default Emphasis	*Sublanguage-specific* *User-System Relationship* *expressions:* *Emphasis:* Usr-Sys-Rel Emphasis higher amplitude
Sublanguage-specific lexicon, expressions and terminology: (ACTION-TYPE, OBJECT-TYPE)	system-service expressions system-intention expressions user-action/intention expressions
Sublanguage-independent *expressions:* *(Greek: Prosodically-determined)* *Emphasis:* Default Emphasis	*Sublanguage-independent* *expressions:* *(Greek: Prosodically-determined)* *Emphasis:* Default Emphasis Lower amplitude
spatial, temporal and quantitative expressions expressions related to manner and quality	spatial, temporal and quantitative expressions expressions related to manner and quality

It can, thus be observed that for Non-Task-related Speech Acts the proposed approach is partially language independent. This is in contrast to the proposed prosodic modeling for Task-related Speech Acts, where the proposed prosodic modeling may act as a Controlled language-like approach. The parameters presented for the prosodic modeling of Non-Task-related Speech Acts may, therefore, only be applied as a "lax" Controlled language-like strategy.

Table 10 summarizes the observed similarities and differences in respect to the relation of prosodic emphasis and word category for the Prosodic Modeling of Task-related and Non-Task-related Speech Acts in Service-oriented Dialogs (Table 10).

Chapter 5

LANGUAGE-SPECIFIC
TONE AND STYLE

Although prosodic emphasis provides the basis for achieving the targeted effect in the sentence's prosodic structure, the appropriate tone of voice in the System's utterances plays a final and decisive role both in respect to Comprehensibility and in respect to User-Friendliness. We note that adaptation and fine-tuning in respect to the appropriate nuance of tone is observed to be easier accomplished by pre-recorded output produced by a trained speaker than by Speech Synthesis.

Regardless of the user-friendly content of the utterance produced, an unfriendly tone neutralizes any attempt aiming to User-friendliness. In contrast to the above-presented specifications based on the role of prosodic emphasis in prosodic modeling, tone cannot be fully specified as a set of stand-alone parameters and is strongly related to the quality of the Speaker's (or the System's) voice and the training (or fine-tuning) of the Speaker (or System).

As a basic framework, the combination of the "Instrument" and "Servant" User-Psychology in relation to Task Type does help eliminate cases in which the System mimics specific male or female prototypes within a culture-specific framework. The characteristics of specific culturally determined male or female prototypes are related to a complex matrix of various features, also associated with tone of voice. In the present approach, the combination of Task Type and the "Instrument" and "Servant" User-Psychology, allows a relatively neutral baseline on which the overall tone of the System's utterances can be adapted, according to preferences of the particular User or User-Group.

However, even in this case, the acceptable tone of voice in the utterances produced by the System's Spoken Output may vary according to culture and language-type. For example, in some languages a characteristically vivid and expressive tone is maintained in many types of transactions and related Speech Acts, such as in spoken Italian. In other languages, such as spoken German, in a considerable number of transactions, a tone associated with reliability and responsibility is preferred. In most cases, at least for the languages and their Native Speakers in Europe, developers in Human-Computer Interaction systems have to balance between a tone associated with reliability, responsibility and, in some task-types, even authority, while at the same time User-friendliness and naturalness must be preserved. This is a necessary process for languages such as Greek, where Positive Politeness markers integrated in the prosodic modeling process prevent a tone associated with reliability and responsibility to be perceived as authoritative and rude by Greek Native Speakers (Alexandris and Fotinea, 2004). On the other hand, some languages, such as the so-called "BBC-English" or "Queen's English" in British English appear to have some "ready-made" varieties in tone and style balancing between the above-described characteristics. The acceptable tone of voice is, therefore, directly related to socio-cultural factors and cannot be excluded from the prosodic modeling process for applications targeted to User-Groups such as the General Public.

Chapter 6

CONCLUSION

The target of the present approach is to provide a general framework of re-usable, transferable and language independent specifications for the Speech Component in Service-Oriented Dialog Systems for the General Public as a user group. It should be stressed that the above-described features constitute basic specifications and are subject to further "streamlining" when processed by prosodic modeling tools.

The present approach concerns specifications based on prosodic modeling directly related to Speech Act type which is, in turn, related to dialog type and dialog structure. This relation is determined by the overall framework of the Parameters (1-5) of the HCI System in respect to the User-System Relationship.

It may, additionally, be noted that the proposed prosodic-emphasis based approach can constitute a stand-alone specification for prosodic modeling, although, it should be taken into account that the overall tone in respect to the mode of articulation plays a decisive role.

In respect to the language-independent feature, the proposed prosodic modeling approach can be characterized as partially language independent, depending on Speech Act type, namely Task-related or Non-Task-related Speech Acts. Specifically, within the framework of the present approach, based on the relation of Speech Act type and Prosodic Modeling, it is observed that Task-related Speech Acts display compatibility in respect to prosodic emphasis and word category in the three languages concerned, namely, English, German and Greek. In English and in German, in contrast to specific word categories in Greek, it is observed that prosodic emphasis does not usually affect the actual semantic content of words.

Contrary to Task-related Speech Acts, it is observed that in the language pairs English, German and Greek, Non-Task-related Speech Acts display partial compatibility in respect to prosodic emphasis and word category. Partial compatibility is shown to result from differences in the morphosyntactic and semantic level (expressions) and is also related to variations in respect to the content and acceptability of the Speech Act in the languages concerned. These parameters influencing the form and content of Non-Task-related Speech Acts are summarized as the Grammatical and Lexical Parameter and the Pragmatic and Sociolinguistic Parameter.

The above-described differences between Task-related Speech Acts and Non-Task-related Speech Acts, at least for the languages concerned, are observed to be related to the typically standard and relatively language-independent content of Task-related Speech Acts, in contrast to Non-Task-related Speech Acts, where the content is often not standard, may be highly dependent on user-requirements and acceptable socio-cultural norms and is, therefore mostly language-dependent.

From the aspect of implementation, in Task-related Speech Acts, where User expectations are predefined and also relatively language and culture independent, the proposed prosodic modeling may act as a Controlled language-like approach applied to facilitate Speech Recognition and semantic processing and to standardize System input and output. We note here that it has been observed that controlled language-like specifications originating from English and German are mostly applicable in Greek (Alexandris, 2009). In contrast to the proposed prosodic modeling for Task-related Speech Acts, the parameters presented for the prosodic modeling of Non-Task-related Speech Acts can be applied as a "lax" Controlled language-like approach. It can, therefore, be concluded that the Controlled language-like specifications of the proposed approach for prosodic modeling can be characterized by features ranging from full to partial reusability and transferability to other applications.

The approaches presented for the prosodic modeling in Service-Oriented HCI Systems, namely the Controlled language-like approach for Task-related Speech Acts and the "lax" Controlled language-like approach for Non-Task-related Speech Acts, can be applied in Work packages for User Requirements and Dialog Modeling. We also note here that the typically standard and relatively language-independent content of Task-related Speech Acts is easily adaptable to the language-independent features typically integrated in an Interlingua (ILT). It may, additionally, be noted here that prosodic emphasis as a pointer to key content in Task-related Speech Acts may help facilitate the transfer process in ILT-based multilingual applications, especially if languages from diverse language families are involved.

As a final note, in respect to the relation of prosody and content of utterance within the framework of Service-Oriented dialogs and from the present data and respective European Union projects, it may be observed that Greek appears to be more sensitive to prosody, where English and German rely more substantially on content such as modifiers and particles. Specifically, from the present data, Prosody is observed to play a more intense role in respect to word semantics and overall User-friendliness in Greek, where in English and in German, both word semantics and User-friendliness are concretely defined and realized by vocabulary. Specifically, it is observed that, in addition to the expressions signaling the User-System Relationship ("Usr-Sys-Rel" words) receiving prosodic emphasis (and resulting to a User-friendly effect), there is an extensive use of modifiers, especially adverbials, (also accompanying most "default-emphasis" words in Task-related Speech Acts) and more extensive use of particles and pragmatically polite expressions.

The relation of prosody, word semantics and overall User-friendliness in Greek, English and in German beyond the framework of Service-Oriented HCI Systems remains an issue for further investigation. However, it may be observed that, in respect to prosodic emphasis, language-specific as well as culture-specific factors play a substantial role in Service-Oriented HCI Systems, at least for the language pair English, German and Greek.

Compatibility with other languages in respect to the present prosodic modeling approach is an issue for further research, especially if the other languages in question display substantial differentiations in respect to the Task-Related and Non-Task-Related Speech Act types and the overall framework of the User-System Relationship.

REFERENCES

Alexandris, C. (2009): A Speech-Act Oriented Approach for User-Interactive Editing and Regulation Processes Applied in Written and Spoken Technical Texts, in: *Human-Computer Interaction. HCI Intelligent Multimodal Interaction Environments*. Vol. 2, LNCS_5611.

Alexandris, C. (2008): Word Category and Prosodic Emphasis in Dialog Modules of Speech Technology Applications. In: Botinis, A. (ed) *Proceedings of the 2nd ISCA Workshop on Experimental Linguistics, ExLing2008*, Athens, Greece, August, pp. 5—8.

Alexandris, C. (2007): "Show and Tell": Using Semantically Processable Prosodic Markers for Spatial Expressions in an HCI System for Consumer Complaints". In: Jacko, J. A. (ed) *Human-Computer Interaction. HCI Intelligent Multimodal Interaction Environment*, vol. 4552/2007, Springer, New York, pp. 13 —22.

Alexandris, C., Fotinea, S-E. (2004): Discourse Particles: Indicators of Positive and Non-Positive Politeness in the Discourse Structure of Dialog Systems for Modern Greek. In: *International Journal for Language Data Processing "Sprache & Datenverarbeitung"*, vol. 1-2/2004, pp. 19-29.

Hausser, R. (2006): A *Computational Model of Natural Language Communication, Interpretation, Inference and Production in Database Semantics*. Springer, Berlin.

Heeman, R., Byron, D., Allen, J. F. (1998): Identifying Discourse Markers in Spoken Dialog. In: *Proceedings of the AAAI Spring Symposium on Applying Machine Learning to Discourse Processing*, Stanford, March 1998 .

Kellner, A. (2004): Dialogsysteme. In: *Computerlinguistik und Sprachtechnologie, Eine Einführung*, Carstensen, K.U., Ebert, C.,

46 Christina Alexandris

Endriss, C., Jekat, S., Klabunde, R., Langer, H. (eds.), 2nd. revised edition, München: Spektrum Akademischer Verlag.

Lehrndorfer A. (1996): *Kontrolliertes Deutsch: Linguistische und Sprachpsychologische Leitlinien für eine (maschniell) kontrollierte Sprache in der technischen Dokumentation.*Narr, Tuebingen.

Malagardi, I. and Alexandris, C. (2009): "Verb Processing in Spoken Commands for Household Security and Appliances", in:. *Universal Access in Human-Computer Interaction.* Vol. 6, LNCS_5615.

Moeller, S. (2005): *Quality of Telephone-Based Spoken Dialogue Systems.* Springer, New York.

Nottas, M., Alexandris, C, Tsopanoglou, A. Bakamidis, S. (2007): *A Hybrid Approach to Dialog Input in the CitzenShield Dialog System for Consumer Complaints.* In: Proceedings of HCI 2007, Beijing China.

Sifianou, M. (2001): *Discourse Analysis. An Introduction.* Athens: Leader Books.

Schilder, F., Habel, C. (2001): From Temporal Expressions to Temporal Information: Semantic tagging of News Messages. In: *Proceedings of the ACL-2001, Workshop on Temporal and Spatial Information Processing*, Pennsylvania, pp.1309-1316.

Smart, J. (2006): SMART Controlled English. In: *Proceedings of the 5th International Workshop on Controlled Language Applications* (CLAW 2006), Cambridge, MA, USA August 12, 2006.

Wiegers, Karl .E. (2005): *Software Requirements*, Redmond, WA: Mircosoft Press.

Wojcik, R.H., Holmback, H. (1996): Getting a Controlled Language Off the Ground at Boeing. In: *Proceedings of CLAW– 1996*, Leuven, Belgium, pp. 22–31.

INDEX

A

achievement, 11, 13, 28
ACL, 46
adaptation, 39
adaptations, 29
ambiguity, 11
amplitude, 26, 29, 30, 31, 37
applications, vii, 1, 4, 5, 11, 12, 24, 25, 27, 28, 29, 33, 40, 42, 43
articulation, 41
authority, 40

B

Beijing, 46
Belgium, 46

C

categorization, 22, 23
category d, 18
children, vii, 1
China, 46
clarity, 11, 17, 28
communication, 3, 17
compatibility, 18, 31, 32, 41, 42
components, 12
construction, 1

crack, 16
cultural norms, 7, 42
culture, vii, 1, 2, 7, 39, 40, 42, 43

D

database, 23
definition, 1
differentiation, 15
directives, 27
discourse, 15, 16
dyslexia, 4

E

emotion, vii, 1
environment, 12
Europe, 40
European Union, 3, 11, 15, 18, 19, 22, 28, 43
execution, 3, 4, 12

F

failure, 8, 25, 32